Nature's Rainbow

Shari Last

Rich reds of a ruby, red apple, and rose.

red snapper

strawberries

macaw

The macaw turns heads wherever he goes.

watermelon

coral

Orange shades in the leaves and produce of fall.

Those bright yellow hues of the sun and sweet fruit,

Lemons that are sour and bumblebees cute.

sapphire

morpho butterfly

In shades of amethyst, lavender, plum, and violet.

Pretty in pink from flamingos to pigs.

No blossom too lovely, no crystal too big.

The dazzling whites of swans, ducks, and mice,

Warm as
sunny daisies
or frosty as ice.

Polar bear

sheep

chicken

alpaca

Natural browns are lovely to see:

owl, cricket, tree, coconut, hedgehog, snail

Lustrous fur, sleek feathers, and the bark of a tree.

Black – so dark it just draws you right in.

We've explored all the colours, one by one.

Now let's find . . .

First published in Great Britain in 2024
by TELL ME MORE Books

Text copyright ©2024 Shari Last
Design copyright ©2024 Shari Last

ISBN: 978-1-917200-08-0

Picture credits: Thanks to baddesigner.

All rights reserved. Without limiting the rights under the copyright reserved above, no part of this publication may be reproduced, stored in, or introduced into a retrieval system, or transmitted, in any form, or by any means (electronic, mechanical, photocopying, recording or otherwise), without the prior written permission of the copyright owner.

WWW.TELLMEMOREBOOKS.COM

www.ingramcontent.com/pod-product-compliance
Lightning Source LLC
Chambersburg PA
CBHW050749110526
44591CB00002B/31